Heroes and Villains of the

WILD WEST

Jesse James

by John Hamilton

ABDO & Daughters
PUBLISHING

Published by Abdo & Daughters, 4940 Viking Dr., Suite 622, Edina, MN 55435.

Copyright ©1996 by Abdo Consulting Group, Inc., Pentagon Tower, P.O. Box 36036, Minneapolis, Minnesota 55435. International copyrights reserved in all countries. No part of this book may be reproduced in any form without written permission from the publisher. Printed in the United States.

Cover Photo by: Bettmann Archive
Inside Photos by:
Bettmann Archive: pp. 5, 6, 11, 12, 15, 16, 19, 27
Wide World Photos: pp. 7, 9
Archive Photos: p. 25
Lemon, John Jay. *The Northfield Tragedy*: pp. 20, 21

Edited by Ken Berg

Library of Congress Cataloging–in–Publication Data
Hamilton, John, 1959–
    Jesse James / written by John Hamilton
        p. cm. — (Heroes & villains of the wild West)
    Includes bibliographical references and index.
    Summary: The life story of Jesse James, famous outlaw of the Old West, from his activities in the Civil War and his career as a bank robber to his demise at the hands of Bob Ford.
    ISBN: 1-56239-559-9
    1. James, Jesse, 1847–1882—Juvenile literature. 2. Outlaws—West (U.S.)—Biography—Juvenile literature. 3. Frontier and pioneer life—West (U.S.)—Juvenile literature. 4. West (U.S.)—History—1860–1890—Juvenile literature. [1. James, Jesse, 1847–1882. 2. Robbers and outlaws. 3. Frontier and pioneer life—West (U.S.) 4. West (U.S.)—History.] I. Title. II. Series.
F594.J27H35 1996
364.1'552'092—dc20   95-25040
[B]   CIP
                                                              AC

Contents

The First Raid

"Give me all your money or I'll blow your head off!" Clay County Savings Bank clerk William Bird stared down the barrel of the Colt pistol aimed at him from the other side of the counter. The tall man holding the gun stood there, his trigger finger twitching. Bird took a step back, afraid for his life. His father, cashier Greenup Bird, looked up from the bank books at his desk. "What's going on?"

Instantly, the bandit and his partner, each dressed in blue soldiers' overcoats, leaped over the counter and trained their revolvers at the two bank employees.

Outside the building, several rough-looking men stood ready, some near the bank entrance and the rest on horseback across the street. They appeared as men accustomed to living in the saddle. It was a cold, gray day on February 13, 1866, in Liberty, Missouri. The men wore long riding coats that hid the pistols strapped to their belts. Nobody took notice as the men waited anxiously.

Back inside, young William Bird was furiously stuffing wheat sacks with $60,000 in cash, gold, and government bonds. The senior Mr. Bird stood, his hands in the air, watching his son empty the vault at gunpoint. He glanced over as one of the robbers, the one with the steely blue eyes, walked up to the older man and aimed his gun at his head. Bird gulped.

Jesse James, 18-year-old farm boy from Clay County, Missouri, Civil War veteran and now first-time bank robber, chuckled. He looked to his older brother, Frank, and displayed the odd sense of humor he would later be known for. Declaring that "the Birds need to be caged," he ordered Greenup Bird into the vault along with his son, and slammed shut the vault door.

Once outside, Frank and Jesse mounted their horses. The gang slowly rode away, seemingly unnoticed. Suddenly, shots rang out. A young college student had been walking to class. One of the robbers noticed the

4

Jesse James as a young man.

lad staring at the gang. Fearing he would raise an alarm, the thief shot him in the chest, killing him instantly. The silence now broken, the horsemen began firing into the air, whooping and hollering, then thundered madly out of town.

A posse quickly gave chase, but the gang's tracks were soon erased when a blinding snowstorm struck the area. It was the first daylight bank robbery in America in peacetime, and it sent shockwaves throughout the countryside. The legacy of Jesse James had begun.

The Clay County Savings Association bank building in Liberty, Missouri. On February 13, 1866, Jesse James and his gang staged the first daylight bank robbery in America in peacetime. They got away with $60,000, a small fortune in those days.

Jesse James as a mature man. The photo's authenticity has been verified by his wife.

American Robin Hood

Has there ever been a desperado so well-known, so etched into our folklore and common image of the American frontier, as Jesse Woodson James, the "Robin Hood" robber who supposedly stole from the rich and gave to the poor? As stories of his adventures passed down from generation to generation, Jesse has become larger than life. But most of the tales told of Jesse James are just that—stories. In truth, Jesse was a killer and thief. During a crime spree that lasted over 15 years, he murdered several innocent people, including unarmed bank tellers, law men, and citizens simply caught in the crossfire.

Jesse James was born in a small log cabin on September 5, 1847, four years after his brother Frank, in Clay County, a farming community in northwestern Missouri. Shortly after his birth, Jesse's father, a Baptist minister, set off for the California gold fields, where he died of pneumonia. Jesse's mother, Zerelda, remarried twice, finally settling down with Dr. Reuben Samuel, a doctor and farmer content to let his wife raise her rambunctious boys the way she pleased.

Not far from the Samuel home lived the boys' cousins: Cole, James, John, and Robert Younger. (They would later team up with Jesse and Frank to form the core of the James-Younger gang.) For the most part, they were good boys, with nothing to hint that they would grow up to be notorious outlaws of the West.

A poster advertising a drama about the life of Jesse James.

The Making of a Criminal

In 1861, the Civil War began. Missouri was a border state with supposed loyalty to the Union, but many people had close ties to the Confederacy. Jesse's mother was a slaveholder, and the family considered themselves Southerners. At the start of the war, Jesse was too young to fight, but brother Frank and cousin Cole Younger joined a new kind of Confederate group called "guerrillas." (Not gorillas.) They fought without rules, using surprise and shock. Their tactics led to much horror and bloodshed. Many thought them criminals, not soldiers.

Yet, at the same time, the people of northern Missouri endured brutality at the hands of Union troops from the north. Once soldiers paid a visit to the Samuel farm, having learned that Frank was a guerrilla member. They tied a rope around Dr. Samuel's neck and jerked him up in the air four times, trying to make the poor doctor tell them where Frank was hiding out. They also pushed around and threatened Jesse's mother, who was pregnant at the time. Then they found young Jesse hiding in the family's cornfield. The soldiers lashed him in the back as he tried to run away. Failing to get their information, the troopers finally left.

After this episode, Jesse joined his brother Frank in the guerrilla forces. Jesse's hatred of the Union military was legendary. One of his first tastes of blood was at the massacre of Centralia, where 75 unarmed Union soldiers were gunned down. Shortly afterwards, the guerrilla forces met Union troops trying to catch the Missourians. The guerrillas turned and charged the federal troops, slaughtering most of them. Jesse killed several men, including the commanding officer. In all, over 100 Union troops died in the bloodbath. Jesse had to wipe blood from his clothes that night. He was only 17.

Frank (center) and Jesse (right) James with a fellow comrade during their soldiering days in the Confederate Army.

Jesse's skill with a horse and gun were well-known throughout the guerrilla camps. His marksmanship was better than most, even those men with more years and experience. He also started showing signs of his leadership ability, which someday would serve him as head of an outlaw gang.

Jesse James' experiences during the Civil War taught him leadership and marksmanship, two skills he would later put to use during his outlaw days.

End of the War

When the Civil War ended, people were uncertain what would happen to the guerrillas. Since they weren't regular military troops, many thought they should be tried as criminals. Some guerrillas were hunted down and simply shot. Jesse and Frank lived in terror. Their home was empty, their parents having been forcefully sent by the government to Nebraska during the war because of the actions of their sons. Finally, in early 1865, a pardon was given. The former guerrillas could go home if they turned themselves in and pledged to live in peace.

When Jesse surrendered, so the story goes, Union troops opened fire, severely wounding him in the chest. He barely escaped, making it to his family in Nebraska. For a time, it looked as if he would die. He begged his mother to take him back to Missouri. "I don't want to die in a Northern state," he said. On the way, the family stopped at his uncle's house in Harlem, Missouri. There he was nursed back to health by his cousin Zerelda (named after his mother). Jesse called her "Zee," and the couple soon fell in love. They became engaged at that time, but wouldn't marry until years later.

Back home in Clay County, the James brothers tended their land, peacefully farming for the next four years. Some say Jesse later turned to a life of crime because of the cruelty of Union soldiers during the Civil War. Others believe it was because of mistreatment by "carpetbaggers" (Northerners with money who controlled things after the war and often took advantage of poor Southerners out of greed and revenge). Jesse himself would later say, "We were driven to it."

But this was probably an excuse to get the law off his back. More likely, Jesse and his followers were like many other former guerrillas in northern Missouri at the time: poor, bored, and aching for a more exciting life in the saddle. As Bob Younger would later say, "We are rough men and used to rough ways."

Outlaws

After the first robbery in Liberty, Missouri, the James gang struck other banks over the next several years, using the same military tactics they learned as Confederate guerrillas. They often rode into town in separate groups. After robbing the bank, they would then shoot into the air and give the Rebel yell, trying to instill terror into the townsfolk. They would then split up again to make their capture more difficult.

On May 22, 1867, Jesse's gang rode into Richmond, Missouri, terrorizing the town and robbing the bank of about $4,000. Three people, including Mayor John Shaw, were killed during the raid. The people of Missouri were outraged. Mob justice reared its ugly head. Several people suspected of being gang members were captured and either hanged or lynched without trial. But the James and Younger brothers escaped.

It was difficult in those days to catch criminals, especially in the wild rural areas. There were no modern scientific methods available, like fingerprints or even photographs of the suspects. Worse, local citizens seldom helped. They saw the lawmen as stooges of the railroads and banks. Friends of the James and Younger brothers often lied to the law or hid the gang at their farms. Others refused to speak out of fear. Whatever the reason, once the gang made it back into the woods and shelter of home territory, catching them was next to impossible.

Up to this point, no one had ever positively identified Jesse as an outlaw—until December 7, 1869. On that day Jesse, his brother Frank, and Cole Younger rode into Gallatin, Missouri, heading for the Davies County Savings Bank. Cashier John Sheets soon found himself faced by a rough-looking, blue-eyed man asking change for a $100 bill. As Sheets reached for his receipt book, the stranger whipped out his Colt revolver and shot Sheets through the head and heart. William McDowell, a bank clerk, bolted for the door amid a hail of bullets. Though wounded, he escaped to raise the alarm. Jesse James reached over the counter and grabbed what money he could, about $500.

A photograph discovered in a New Mexico saloon that shows Jesse (right) and Frank James (left), together with their mother in the center.

Once on the street, the bandits met a fierce resistance from angry citizens. Jesse caught his foot in his stirrup and was dragged by his horse almost 40 feet before he could get free. Frank stopped to help. Jesse leaped up in the saddle behind his brother and the two galloped out of town.

The citizens of Gallatin screamed for justice. This time they had solid evidence: Jesse's horse. Detectives soon pointed the finger at the Samuel farm. As one newspaper predicted, "Should the miscreants be overtaken it is not probable that a jury will be required to try them. They will be shot down in their tracks."

A group of well-armed citizens surrounded the farm. As they closed in, the door to the barn suddenly opened and out burst Frank and Jesse James on horseback, riding away for their lives. Later, Jesse would say his horse found in Gallatin had been stolen, and that he was innocently farming at the time of the holdup. Jesse and Frank fled, he explained, because they didn't want to be lynched by a mob. Given the hanging mood in the countryside, he may have been wise to run away. He wrote many letters to editors of newspapers professing his innocence, claiming he couldn't turn himself in because he would never get a fair trial.

Jesse's name nevertheless would now be connected to numerous robberies in Missouri and neighboring states. The law would be hot on his trail from now on. Several attempts were made by Pinkertons, private investigators hired by the railroads, to track down Jesse and his gang. Most attempts ended in tragedy, with the Pinkertons getting the worst end of the deal.

The holdups continued. In addition to banks, Jesse now targeted trains and stagecoaches. Trains usually carried large sums of payroll money, ripe for the picking. Jesse became more confident with each heist. By now Jesse James had become an embarrassment to politicians in Missouri, which to their shame was known as the "Bandit State." The hunt intensified.

A popular lithograph showing Jesse James attacking a posse that has set out to capture him.

The James Gang liked to rob trains because "iron horses" often carried large sums of gold and payroll money.

Jesse Marries

Lawmen and Pinkertons stalked the countryside, waiting for Jesse James to show his face. But, suddenly, the robberies stopped. After years of living on the run, Jesse married his cousin Zee in Kansas City on April 23, 1874. Jesse said this about the marriage: "On the 23rd of April, 1874, I was married to Miss Zee Mimms, of Kansas City, and at the house of a friend there. About fifty of our mutual friends were present on the occasion, and quite a noted Methodist minister performed the ceremonies. We had been engaged for nine years, and through good and evil report, and not withstanding the lies that had been told upon me and the crimes laid at my door, her devotion to me has never wavered for a moment. You can say that both of us married for love, and that there cannot be any sort of doubt about our marriage being a happy one."

Jesse was still trying to get the law off his back with two tired arguments: 1) he was innocent of most of the crimes he was accused of and could never get a fair trial; and 2) any crimes he did commit he did so out of revenge for the mistreatment of the South during and after the Civil War.

His marriage helped his cause. As one newspaper declared in announcing his wedding, "All the world loves a lover." After quietly settling in a small cabin near Kearney, Missouri, Zee and Jesse had two children, Jesse, Jr. and Mary. Yet the manhunt persisted.

On the night of January, 26, 1875, a group of Pinkertons and local lawmen crept up on Jesse's mother's cabin, thinking the outlaw was holed up at the Samuel farm. They tossed a smoke grenade through a window. The night sky lit up with a thunderous explosion. Screams echoed from inside the house. Something had gone terribly wrong.

The smoke grenade had landed in the fireplace, where it exploded like a bomb. The blast killed Jesse's eight-year-old half brother, Archie, and severely wounded his mother. (Her right arm later had to be amputated.) The incident angered people all over the country. Whether or not Jesse had committed the robberies he was accused of, murdering an innocent child and maiming an old woman was too much for most folks to take.

Support for Jesse grew, especially in the newspapers. The Pinkertons were branded "dastardly dogs who were hunting human flesh for hire." For a time, politicians in Missouri tried to pass an amnesty bill to pardon Jesse and his gang, but it never got enough votes. One night in April of 1875, Daniel Askew, a neighbor of the Samuel's who was suspected of helping the Pinkertons, was gunned down. Most thought Jesse did the deed out of revenge. Talk of amnesty ended, and the robberies resumed.

The James residence in Clay County, Missouri. The fenced-in area in the foreground is the spot where Jesse James was buried before his body was moved to the Kearney, Missouri, cemetery.

The Great Northfield Raid

On September 7, 1876, eight men wearing linen dusters rode into the town of Northfield, Minnesota. The men were Jesse and Frank James, Cole, Jim, and Bob Younger, Charlie Pitts, Clell Miller and Bill Chadwell. That day they began the raid that would nearly destroy the James-Younger gang.

Jesse, Bob Younger and Charlie Pitts entered the First National Bank of Northfield around two o'clock in the afternoon. The others waited outside, keeping guard. J.A. Allen, owner of a hardware store, noticed activity around the bank. Upon investigating, he was grabbed by Clell Miller and warned to keep his mouth shut. Allen broke free and ran away, yelling, "Get your guns, boys! They're robbing the bank!"

Citizens of Northfield, Minnesota, fight back against the James gang.

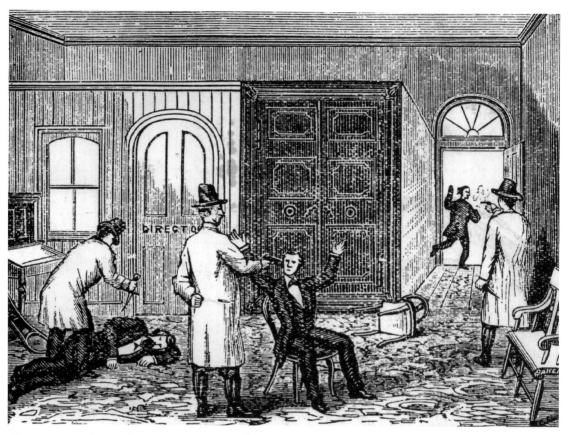

Gang members Jesse James, Bob Younger, and Charlie Pitts attempting to rob the First National Bank of Northfield, Minnesota. Bank employees Joseph Heywood, A.E. Bunker, and F. J. Wilcox refused to open the safe. Bunker, right, escaped but was shot through the shoulder. Heywood, left, was shot dead by the robbers.

The bandits, their cover blown, mounted their horses and thundered up and down the street, shooting and yelling, trying to terrorize the town. Instead, the citizens of Northfield fought back with whatever they could get their hands on, including pistols, rifles, shotguns, even rocks from the dirt road. A Scandinavian immigrant who didn't speak English was gunned down in the street, not understanding the warning to take cover.

Meanwhile, inside the bank, things were going badly. "Open that safe quick or I'll blow your head off," Jesse said, aiming his revolver at the cashier, Joseph Heywood. Heywood refused. (Actually, the safe was already open; the bandits forgot to check.) Frustrated by the man's stubbornness, Charlie Pitts cut Heywood's throat with his knife, wounding him slightly. Another cashier, A. E. Bunker, made a dash for the door. Pitts chased him, shooting after the terrified man, but the cashier escaped. At this point, Pitts noticed the chaos outside. He turned back, said, "The game's up!" and then ran outside.

Jesse and Bob Younger followed after scooping up a small amount of money in the cash drawer. Then one of them turned, faced Heywood, and put a bullet in his head. It was never learned which man committed this act, but it would later outrage citizens everywhere for the cowardly deed it was.

When Jesse and Bob Younger got to the street, the battle was in full swing. Gunfire was coming fast and with deadly accuracy. The gang attempted to make a quick getaway, but the street would hold death for two of them. Clell Miller was shot square in the face with a shotgun, and Bill Chadwell was plugged right through the heart. Another bandit's horse was shot out from under him. Most of the rest of the gang were also wounded in the deadly crossfire. The citizens of Northfield had stood their ground and won.

Once safely outside of town, Jesse and Frank decided to split up with the Youngers to avoid capture. Bob Younger was severely wounded, slowing the group.

Two weeks later a posse caught up with the Youngers, and a fierce showdown took place on the Minnesota prairie near St. James. Afterwards, Charlie Pitts lay dead, and the three Younger brothers severely wounded. The Youngers were later sent to Minnesota's Stillwater State Prison.

The Northfield Raid

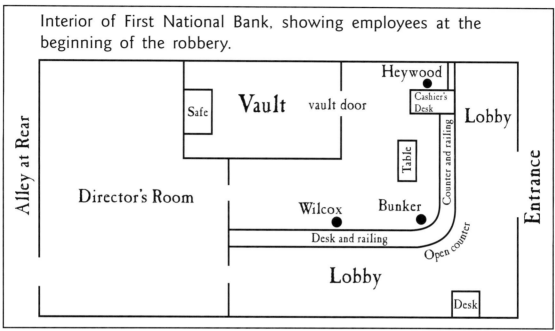

Interior of First National Bank, showing employees at the beginning of the robbery.

Heywood

Cashier's Desk

Vault — vault door

Safe

Lobby

Alley at Rear

Director's Room

Table

Counter and railing

Wilcox

Bunker

Desk and railing

Open counter

Lobby

Entrance

Desk

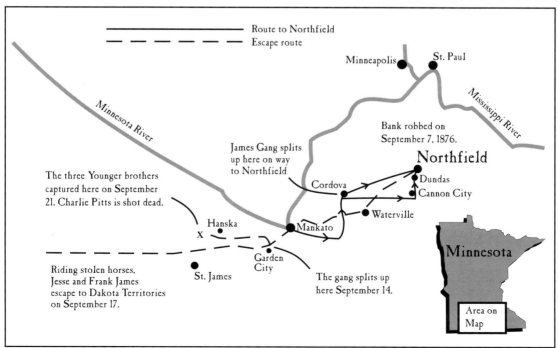

Route to Northfield
Escape route

Minneapolis St. Paul

Mississippi River

Minnesota River

Bank robbed on September 7, 1876.

James Gang splits up here on way to Northfield

Northfield

Cordova Dundas
Cannon City

The three Younger brothers captured here on September 21. Charlie Pitts is shot dead.

Waterville

Hanska

X

Mankato

Minnesota

Riding stolen horses, Jesse and Frank James escape to Dakota Territories on September 17.

St. James

Garden City

The gang splits up here September 14.

Area on Map

23

The Death of Jesse James

Frank and Jesse barely escaped to Missouri, fleeing through the Dakota Territories and Iowa before making it home. The entire country was in an uproar over the raid in Northfield. People wanted Jesse captured, dead or alive.

Jesse and Frank laid low, managing to stay out of trouble for three years. But in 1879, Jesse formed a new gang, and was soon doing what he knew best: robbing banks and trains. The brutality of a train stickup outside of Winston, Missouri, prompted Governor Thomas Crittenden to offer a reward of $10,000. It was a huge sum for those times. Jesse's days were numbered.

On the morning of April 3, 1882, Jesse met with two gang members, Bob and Charlie Ford, in his new home in St. Joseph, Missouri. Jesse was now living under the alias of Mr. Thomas Howard. "Mr. Howard" wanted to talk with the Ford brothers about robbing the Platte County Bank of a fortune he thought would let them all finally retire from a life of crime.

Putting his gunbelt on a chair, Jesse turned his back on the Fords to straighten a picture on the wall. He let his guard down for one fatal moment. Bob Ford stepped up, aimed his pistol at the back of Jesse's head, and fired, killing him instantly. The brothers ran from the house, Bob screaming, "I killed him! I killed Jesse James!"

One of many reward posters calling for the capture of Jesse James.

Reaction from the public was immediate and sharp: the shooting of Jesse James in the back, while unarmed, was a cowardly act of betrayal. Instead of the fame and fortune Bob Ford expected, he got nothing but scorn and ridicule. A song written about Jesse the day after his death included these lines:

"Jesse had a wife to mourn for his life,
Two children, they were brave,
But that dirty little coward that shot Mister Howard,
Has laid poor Jesse in his grave."

Five months later, Frank James surrendered to the law, tired of living the life of an outlaw. The public, so outraged by the way Jesse died, was in no mood to throw his brother in jail. Frank was never convicted after a series of trials, and returned to his farm to live without incident until his death in 1915.

Bob Younger died in prison. His two brothers were paroled in 1901. Jim committed suicide after being rejected by a woman he had courted while in jail. Cole Younger, the last of the original gang members, returned to Missouri to live out the rest of his life peacefully, finally dying of a heart attack in 1916. The James-Younger gang was no more. But Jesse's name would live on.

Robert Ford, killer of Jesse James.

The Wild West of Jesse James

Minnesota

Stillwater Prison

Northfield•

•St. James

South Dakota

Iowa

Nebraska

St. Joseph•   •Gallatin

Liberty•   •Richmond

•Kansas City   •Centralia

Kansas

Missouri

Glossary

amnesty

A general pardon for criminals or offenders by a government. By 1875, there was a great deal of support for Jesse James, especially in the newspapers, which wrote of him more as a folk hero than a criminal. Politicians in Missouri tried to pass a law granting Jesse amnesty for his crimes. But then, in April of 1875, a neighbor of the James' was brutally gunned down for being a suspected helper of Pinkerton detectives. Most people suspected Jesse of pulling the trigger. Talk of amnesty for Jesse and his gang soon ended.

carpetbagger

A Northerner who went to the South during the Reconstruction period after the American Civil War. They were called carpetbaggers because they sometimes carried their belongings in suitcases or sacks made of carpet. Some carpetbaggers were members of government agencies sent to help reconstruct the South; some came on their own to help newly freed African Americans; others were dishonest people hoping to benefit financially or politically. Carpetbaggers had a Southern counterpart, called scalawags. Both were hated by most white Southerners.

Civil War

The war fought in the United States between Union forces (the North) and the Confederacy (the South), between 1861 and 1865. The dispute over whether or not people should own slaves was a major cause of the war.

Colt

A type of pistol commonly used in the Old West. The full tradename is Colt's Revolver. It was developed by Samuel Colt (1814-1862), American inventor and manufacturer of firearms. The Colt was a practical and reliable weapon, and was in great demand in the West and other parts of the country. Anyone who could pull a trigger could now defend themselves in the many lawless regions of the West. A popular saying at the time was, "God created man, but Sam Colt made them equal!"

Pinkerton, Allan (1819–1884)

Scottish-born American detective and Civil War spy. In 1850 he started Pinkerton's National Detective Agency. He became famous after discovering a plot to murder Abraham Lincoln in 1861. During the Civil War he organized the Secret Service of the U.S. Army. The Pinkerton National Detective Agency struck fear into many robbers because of its tireless and thorough tracking down of criminals. The agency's motto was, "We never sleep."

posse

A number of citizens who are given legal authority to round up criminals.

shotgun

A shoulder-held firearm that shoots steel or lead pellets through a smooth bore. Commonly used in hunting birds. Shotguns are also sometimes preferred by lawmen and robbers because they are powerful weapons with a wide blast area, making it easier to hit a moving target than with a pistol, especially at close range.

Bibliography

Encyclopaedia Britannica, Volume V, p. 510.

Flanagan, Mike. *Out West.* New York: Harry N. Abrams, Inc., 1987.

Horan, James D. *The Outlaws: The Authentic Wild West.* New York: Crown Publishers, Inc., 1977.

Huntington, George. *Robber and Hero.* St. Paul: Minnesota Historical Society Press, 1986.

Jordan, Robert Paul. *The Civil War.* Washington, D.C.: National Geographic Special Publications, 1969.

Love, Robertus. *The Rise and Fall of Jesse James.* Lincoln, NE: University of Nebraska Press, 1990.

Nash, Jay Robert. *Bloodletters and Badmen.* New York: M. Evans and Company, 1973.

Ross, James R. *I, Jesse James.* Dragon Publishing Corp., 1988.

Settle, William A. Jr.. *Jesse James Was His Name.* Lincoln, NE: University of Nebraska Press, 1966.

Steele, Phillip W. *Jesse and Frank James: The Family History.* Gretna, LA: Pelican Publishing Company, 1987.

The Northfield Bank Raid. Northfield, MN: Northfield News, Inc., 1980.

Index